EXPLORING SCIENCE

NATURAL RESOURCES

USING AND PROTECTING EARTH'S SUPPLIES

BY DARLENE R. STILLE

Content Adviser: Jim Walker, Professor of Geology and
Environmental Geosciences, Northern Illinois University

Science Adviser: Terrence E. Young Jr., M.Ed., M.L.S.,
Jefferson Parish (Louisiana) Public School System

Reading Adviser: Susan Kesselring, M.A., Literacy Educator,
Rosemount-Apple Valley-Eagan (Minnesota) School District

COMPASS POINT BOOKS · MINNEAPOLIS, MINNESOTA

Compass Point Books • 3109 West 50th Street, #115 • Minneapolis, MN 55410

Visit Compass Point Books on the Internet at *www.compasspointbooks.com*
or e-mail your request to *custserv@compasspointbooks.com*

Photographs ©: Mike Zens/Corbis, cover; Brand X Pictures, 4; Lowell Georgia/Corbis, 5, 27; Photodisc, 6, 11, 12, 16, 33; North Wind Picture Archives, 7; Lester V. Bergman/Corbis, 9; Brian Parker/Tom Stack & Associates, 10; Corbis, 13, 26, 28, 36; Creatas, 15; Jim Baron/The Image Finders, 17; Richard Hamilton Smith, 19, 20; Hulton Archive/Getty Images, 22, 30–31; Vince Streano/Corbis, 23; Arthur Hill/Visuals Unlimited, 25; Mark Allen Stack/Tom Stack & Associates, 32; Alan Schein Photography/Corbis, 34; Koichi Kamoshida/Getty Images, 35; Image Ideas, 37; Chinch Gryniewicz; Ecoscene/Corbis, 38; Stephanie Maze/Corbis, 40; LINK/Visuals Unlimited, 42; John Elk III, 44; Barbara Davidson/Dallas Morning News/Corbis, 46.

Art Director: Keith Griffin
Managing Editor: Catherine Neitge

Editor: Nadia Higgins
Photo Researcher: Marcie C. Spence
Designer/Page production: The Design Lab
Lead Designer: Jaime Martens
Illustrator: Farhana Hossain
Educational Consultant: Diane Smolinski

Library of Congress Cataloging-in-Publication Data
Stille, Darlene R.
   Natural resources : using and protecting Earth's supplies / by Darlene R. Stille.
      p. cm. — (Exploring science)
   Includes bibliographical references and index.
   ISBN 0-7565-0856-8 (hardcover)
   1. Natural resources—Juvenile literature. I. Title. II. Series.
   HC85.S75 2005
   333.7—dc22   2004019416

Printed in the United States of America

About the Author

Darlene R. Stille is a science writer and the author of more than 70 books for young people. When she was in high school, she fell in love with science. While attending the University of Illinois, she discovered that she also loved writing. She was fortunate to find a career as an editor and writer that allowed her to combine both of her interests. Darlene Stille now lives and writes in Michigan.

TABLE OF CONTENTS

A World of Natural Resources

WATER SPILLING from the tap. Black soil crumbling in a garden. Trees silently making oxygen. Sun, wind, air. Our very existence depends on these and other natural resources—as do our comforts and our pleasures.

A natural resource is any substance found in nature that people use. There are hundreds, if not thousands, of kinds of natural resources. They can be as different from each other as a blade of grass and a granite boulder.

Over thousands of years, people have learned to use more and more natural resources to make life easier. Today, people in

Trees—and even sunlight—are two examples of natural resources.

industrialized countries warm their houses with the push of a button. We step on a pedal and a car takes us wherever we want to go. We flick a switch and electric lights come on.

The warmth of a house and the power of an automobile come from the natural resource oil, or petroleum. Even crinkly plastic grocery bags are made from petroleum drilled from deep inside the earth. The electricity that surges into homes and offices may originate from another natural resource, coal.

Some natural resources are easy to recognize, such as sun, wind, and soil. They are the things of our everyday lives. We may never have seen other natural resources such as coal or crude oil. Yet both coal and oil power almost everything around us. Though we feel the constant effects of these natural resources, most of us aren't involved in collecting or preparing them. They seem to come to us with no effort at all.

However, these "effortless" natural resources pose a great challenge to our society. We are using coal and oil much faster

Crude oil spurts out of a well.

than nature can replace them—which means they could run out in our lifetime or that of the next generation or the next. How will people get to work without gas for their cars? How will they run computers without coal to make electricity?

These are some of the most important questions that scientists and public policy officials are working to address. As they research ways to reduce our use of and our need for natural resources such as coal and oil, they rely on us to learn about the complex issues surrounding Earth's scarce supplies.

What are the natural resources we use most? What for? How do our daily choices impact the quality and supply of Earth's natural resources? Understanding these and other issues will help prepare us for future changes in how we use natural resources.

FAST FACT: Petroleum, or crude oil, is also called black gold because it is one of the most valuable natural resources used today.

A man inspects coal at a coal mine.

Natural Resources and the American Pioneers

"Westward ho!" called the leaders of the wagon trains. Long lines of covered wagons set off across North America's Great Plains. Thousands of pioneers in the 1800s went looking for a better life out West.

They carried tools such as saws, axes, hammers, shovels, and plows. They needed these tools to access the natural resources that explorers had found in the plains and hills far away.

Settlers had been moving westward and displacing the native population since the Revolutionary War ended in 1783. First they moved into the areas that are now Kentucky, Tennessee, Ohio, Indiana, Michigan, and Illinois. There they found an abundance of natural resources. They found dense forests filled with wild animals, and clean lakes and rivers filled with fish. They hunted and fished. They cleared the trees and planted crops on the good soil.

Farmland was the main natural resource used by the early pioneers. Farmers in the South planted cotton. Farmers on the Great Plains planted corn and wheat. As land was settled, newcomers had to move farther west.

text continued on page 8

Pioneers clear trees to make way for a farm.

continued from page 7

Pioneers and settlers also discovered coal in Pennsylvania, Virginia, and Illinois. They found iron ore in Minnesota and copper ore in Arizona. They found oil in Oklahoma and Texas. These natural resources became the raw materials for goods made by factories.

Today, the United States is still rich in natural resources. These natural resources have helped make the country one of the wealthiest nations on Earth.

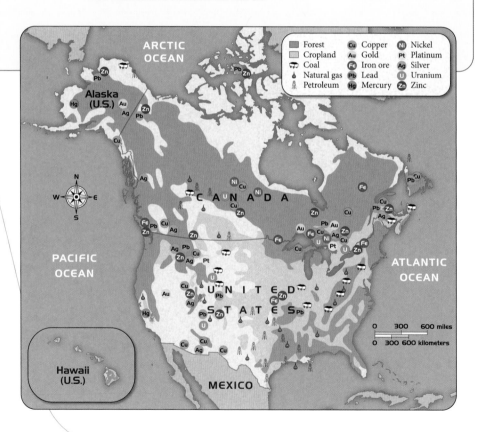

A map showing important natural resources in the United States and Canada

CHAPTER TWO

Living or Nonliving? Renewable or Nonrenewable?

ONE WAY to sort natural resources is to think of them as living resources (such as plants and animals) and nonliving resources (such as soil, air, and water). Living natural resources include forests, which can be harvested for wood. Fish, deer, birds, prairie grasses, and other wild plants and animals are common and useful natural resources, too. These plants and animals can be a direct or indirect source of food.

Natural Resources in a Tiny World

There is a world so tiny that you can see it only through a microscope. Living natural resources are important in this small world. Bacteria, yeasts, and other microscopic organisms use natural resources. Your body is a resource for certain kinds of bacteria. "Good" kinds of bacteria live in your intestines and help you digest food. "Bad" bacteria can get into your body and make you ill.

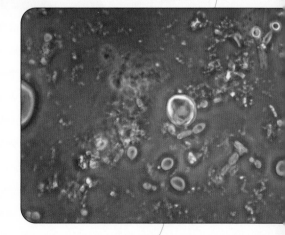

Bacteria in the soil make chemicals that help plants grow. People also use bacteria and yeast as raw materials for making cheese, beer, wine, and even medicines. They use yeast in baking bread.

An enlarged image of baker's yeast, the ingredient that causes bread dough to rise

Another way to categorize natural resources is to think of them as renewable and nonrenewable. Renewable resources are those that get replaced about as fast as we can use them. Most kinds of living natural resources fit into this category, as do nonliving resources such as air and sunlight. Nonrenewable resources, such as coal and oil, get used up faster than they can be replaced and will almost certainly run out one day.

However, the line between renewable and nonrenewable is often fuzzy. Whether or not a resource is truly renewable depends a lot on human behavior. For example, how do we classify species

The Przewalski's horse is an example of a natural resource that has gone from renewable to nonrenewable. It no longer exists in the wild.

of animals that have gone extinct because their habitats have been destroyed by pollution or other kinds of human interference? We can no longer call these animals renewable resources. What happens when forests are cut down so fast that the land they grew on dries up and turns to desert? The possibility for new forests on that land—and the plants and animals that depended on that forest habitat—is gone forever.

The land is threatened when a forest is completely cut down, as this one has been.

CHAPTER THREE

SO THE TERMS *renewable* and *nonrenewable* are general categories. Perhaps the best way to think of a renewable resource is one that can be renewable if it is properly managed. Air, water, soil, and sunlight all fit into this category. All life on Earth depends on these four most vital natural resources.

AIR EVERYWHERE

Plants and animals that live on land need air to survive. During photosynthesis, plants use carbon dioxide, one of air's gases, to make food. Then plants give off oxygen, the life-giving gas that

Divers breathe compressed air from tanks strapped to their backs.

people and other animals need for breathing. People and animals, in turn, give off carbon dioxide when they exhale, or breathe out.

Air can also be a raw material. Divers use "stuffed," or compressed, air in tanks to breathe underwater. The gases in air can also be separated and used individually. Because it burns easily, hydrogen gas has many uses in industry. Helium pumped into a balloon makes the balloon float upward because helium gas is lighter than air.

We will never run out of air, but air pollution makes air unsafe to breathe. Exhaust fumes from automobiles are the leading source of air pollution. Furnaces and air conditioners together make up the second biggest cause, while oil refineries and other factories contribute significantly as well. Since laws such as the

An oil refinery is a cause of air pollution.

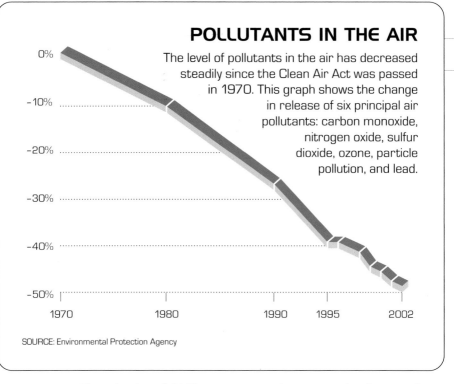

POLLUTANTS IN THE AIR

The level of pollutants in the air has decreased steadily since the Clean Air Act was passed in 1970. This graph shows the change in release of six principal air pollutants: carbon monoxide, nitrogen oxide, sulfur dioxide, ozone, particle pollution, and lead.

0%
-10%
-20%
-30%
-40%
-50%

1970   1980   1990   1995   2002

SOURCE: Environmental Protection Agency

Clean Air Act of 1970 were put in place, air quality has greatly improved. Even so, polluted air contributes to asthma and other lung diseases. It might cause cancer and birth defects. It harms soil, which threatens crops and livestock.

WATER IN YOUR LIFE

Almost three-quarters of Earth's surface is covered with water. More than 97 percent of that water is salty ocean water, and another 2 percent is frozen (mostly at the North Pole and the South Pole). That means less than 1 percent of Earth's water—found in lakes, rivers, and underground chambers—is usable water for drinking. All animals and plants that live on land rely on this fresh water supply for survival.

Only a small percentage of the water we use is for everyday needs such as drinking, bathing, and washing clothes. Factories use enormous amounts of water in manufacturing products. Farmers often use systems of ditches and pipes to irrigate, or bring water to, dry fields.

Water is also an important source of energy. Since the earliest days, people have found ways to use, or harness, the energy in water rushing through rivers or dropping in waterfalls. Today, dams at hydroelectric power plants harness the energy in falling water to generate electricity.

The amount of water on Earth has been fairly consistent over time. Earth recycles its water over and over. The water that you used to shower and brush your teeth this morning has started on a long journey through the water cycle. It will find its way to lakes and rivers and finally to the ocean. Ocean water evaporates and falls back to Earth as rain or snow. Then it begins the journey all over again.

Like air, however, water is not without its problems. Groundwater resources (water found underground) are being used up too quickly, making these important supplies of fresh

An irrigation system brings water to a field.

water nonrenewable. Furthermore, not all places on Earth provide the same amount of fresh water. There is plenty of fresh water in the Great Lakes, for example, but little in the Sahara Desert. Droughts caused by long periods with no rainfall also put water supplies in danger.

Water pollution is another major concern. Throughout history, people have seen what can happen when water becomes so polluted that it is unsafe to drink. Long ago, water polluted with human and animal wastes caused deadly diseases such as typhoid and cholera. Good sewer systems helped clean up this problem. Water treatment plants also add chemicals that kill any leftover germs.

Most water pollution today is caused by chemicals used in farming and industry. Sometimes factories dump chemicals into lakes or rivers. Chemical fertilizers and pesticides run off farmland and into rivers and streams. Oil spills from tankers

Workers clean up an oil spill.

Water Power Through the Ages

People have been making use of water's power for thousands of years. Around the 100s B.C., ancient inventors built the first water wheels next to streams or rivers. Rushing water turned the wheel. The wheel turned simple machinery that ground grain. Later inventors built better water wheels and bigger mills for grinding grain. They used water to power sawmills for cutting lumber.

Early American settlers in the 1600s built dams across rivers. Mill owners used the water falling over the dam to operate their mills. In the late 1800s, engineers designed the first hydroelectric power plants.

A water wheel similar to those used to power mills in the 1800s can kill fish and other ocean animals for miles around. Since the 1970s, the laws to protect our water from being polluted have gotten more and more strict.

SOIL: A SPECIAL CASE

Soil is made up of water, air spaces, and tiny particles of sand, clay, silt, and bits of dead plants and animals. Soil that is rich in decaying plants and animals is best for growing farm crops.

Soil can be considered both renewable and nonrenewable. Soil is often considered nonrenewable because it can take thousands of years for soil to form from weathered rocks and decayed plants and animals. Soil is hard to protect, too. It can easily be blown away by strong winds. It can wash away with heavy rains. Poor farming methods can damage soil to the point where it is unusable. In places where there is poor soil, people often starve to death.

Soil can be considered renewable, however, because there is much that can be done to protect it. Planting trees helps prevent erosion. Tree roots hold the soil so that water and wind cannot carry it away. Adding fertilizer (chemicals or decayed plants and animals) can keep soil from "wearing out" or becoming infertile. Some crops planted year after year take nutrients out of the soil and make it infertile. Rotating crops, meaning planting different kinds of crops, can also keep soil from wearing out. For example,

a farmer might plant corn one year and alfalfa the next year. Corn takes a nutrient called nitrogen away from soil. Alfalfa adds nitrogen to the soil.

THE SUN: SOURCE OF ALL ENERGY

You could think of sunlight as being Earth's most powerful natural resource. It is the source of all the energy on Earth. The energy that began in the sun has transferred into all other forms of energy, including food, wind, and even coal and oil.

Some of this farmland has been left unplanted, or fallow, in order to keep the soil from wearing out. Rows of trees offer a barrier to wind erosion.

For example, plants use sunlight to make food. Plants become food for animals. Plants and animals become food for you.

The sun warms Earth and the air around it. When it meets cooler air, warm air makes the wind blow. Warm air makes water evaporate and fall back to Earth as rain or snow.

Energy from the sun is even trapped in organisms (plants and other living things) that died millions of years ago in swamps and oceans. Coal, petroleum, and natural gas formed from these ancient organisms. Because they are made from the remains of ancient organisms, coal, petroleum, and natural gas are called fossil fuels. Fossil fuels produce about 86 percent of the energy used in the world today.

FAST FACT: Sunlight has not always been so bright. According to one scientific theory called the Faint Young Sun Hypothesis, the amount of sunlight reaching Earth billions of years ago was much less than it is now.

No life on Earth could survive without the sun.

CHAPTER FOUR

Nonrenewable Natural Resources: Fossil Fuels

EVERY DAY, fossil fuels are forming as organisms in swamps and oceans die and decay. However, these organisms will not become coal, petroleum, or natural gas for millions and millions of years. Earth's supply of fossil fuels is getting used up quickly. Energy experts believe we will start running out of petroleum in around 2050. They think there is enough coal and natural gas to last more than 200 years.

HOW DID FOSSIL FUELS BECOME SO IMPORTANT?

The story of fossil fuels began long before dinosaurs walked on Earth. Geologists think that some of the fossil fuels we use today formed as long as 400 million years ago. Dinosaurs lived from about 248 million to 65 million years ago.

People paid little attention to fossil fuels until the Industrial Revolution, which began in the late 1700s. Before then, most things people used were made at home by hand. The Industrial Revolution marked the rise of factories, where mass quantities of goods could be made by machines. These machines required huge amounts of energy—and this energy was found in the form of powerful fossil fuels.

The Steam Engine

The Industrial Revolution began in large part because of the invention of the steam engine. In 1769, a Scottish engineer named James Watt designed a steam engine powerful enough to drive big machines at factories.

To operate a steam engine, water had to be heated to make steam. Coal was a good fuel for doing this job. At first, coal was the most important fossil fuel. Later, engines were invented that ran on oil or gas.

One of James Watt's steam engines, which gave rise to factories and the Industrial Revolution

WHERE DOES COAL COME FROM?

Coal comes from plants that grew in ancient swamps. The plants died and dropped to the bottom of the swamp. The dead plants made layers that hardened as millions of years went by. The layers turned into peat. Millions of more years passed. Layers of rock built up over the peat. Pressure from the rock layers made the peat harden into black or brown coal.

People access coal through either strip mines or underground mines. Strip mines reach coal that is close to the surface, while underground mines reach coal deeper down. In strip mines, huge power shovels scrape away, or "strip," soil and rocks until the coal is exposed. Other huge machines dig out the coal and put it in trucks or train cars. Strip-mining companies must replace the soil and rocks after they have removed the coal.

Underground mines are made of shafts and tunnels. Miners use explosives and giant machines to drill out the coal. They send the coal to the surface on conveyor belts or in special, small train cars.

A coal miner at work in an underground mine

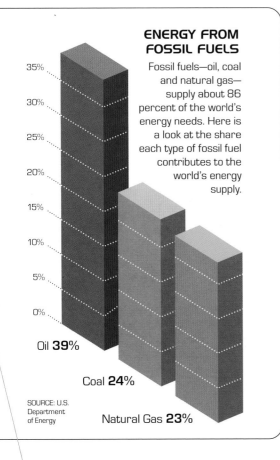

ENERGY FROM FOSSIL FUELS

Fossil fuels—oil, coal and natural gas—supply about 86 percent of the world's energy needs. Here is a look at the share each type of fossil fuel contributes to the world's energy supply.

35%
30%
25%
20%
15%
10%
5%
0%

Oil **39%**

Coal **24%**

SOURCE: U.S.
Department
of Energy

Natural Gas **23%**

HOW IS COAL USED?

Maybe you have never seen a piece of coal. Yet you probably make use of coal every day. This is because many electric power plants burn coal. In fact, power plants burn most of the coal mined in the United States. The burning coal heats water to make steam. Steam drives machines that generate the electricity you use to light your house and run your electric appliances.

FAST FACT: The Chinese in the 300s were the first people known to have strip mines. Europeans began to strip-mine coal in the 1200s.

Mining Ores

Rocks called ores are important nonrenewable resources. Ores are rich in metals such as iron, copper, lead, zinc, silver, nickel, and mercury. Ore deposits usually run in veins through other rock. The veins can be just a few inches or hundreds of feet thick. Miners can scoop up ore that lies near the surface. They dig mine shafts to reach ore that is deep underground.

Ores are the raw materials for all kinds of manufactured products, including construction materials (iron nails and bolts; copper plumbing and electrical wiring), batteries, jewelry, paints, and automotive products.

Uranium ore is of particular importance. Uranium is the radioactive fuel used in nuclear power plants. Nuclear power plants get energy from splitting the centers, or nuclei, of uranium atoms. The energy heats water to make steam. The steam turns big machines called turbines and generators, which make electricity. Nuclear power plants create huge amounts of energy, but they also create hazardous waste products.

Uranium ore is the radioactive fuel used at nuclear power plants.

Coal also has other uses. Many people in the United States once used coal to heat their homes. Homes in parts of Asia and Europe still use coal for heat.

Coal is also burned to make iron and steel. Chemicals called ammonia and coal tar come from coal. Companies use these chemicals as raw materials for making dyes, drugs, fertilizers, and coatings for roofs.

FAST FACT: Power plants that burn coal generate more than half the electricity used in the United States.

A coal-burning power plant provides electricity for an entire city or region.

WHERE DO PETROLEUM AND NATURAL GAS COME FROM?

Petroleum and natural gas were created by similar geological processes. Petroleum, however, is a thick, dark brown or greenish liquid, while natural gas is a mixture of methane and other gases. Natural gas is not to be confused with "gas" as in *gasoline,* the fuel used to run cars.

Geologists think that petroleum and natural gas probably came from tiny animals and plants called plankton. The plankton lived in the ocean millions of years ago. The plankton died and fell to the bottom of the sea. Layer after layer of sediment (sand and mud) piled up above the dead plankton. Over time, the sediments formed layers of sedimentary rock.

The top layers of sedimentary rock pressed down on the layers below. The bottom layers sank deep into the earth, where it is very hot. The high temperatures inside the earth and pressure from the heavy rock above turned some of the dead plankton into dark, sticky crude oil and some into natural gas. Over time, some of the crude oil and natural gas seeped up through rocks and made deposits near the earth's surface.

A petroleum sample from an oil well

FAST FACT: In ancient times, lightning may have struck natural gas coming out of the ground and set it on fire. Imagine what prehistoric people thought when they saw fire coming out of the earth! Ancient Persians worshipped these fires.

HOW DO WE USE PETROLEUM TODAY?

Petroleum is one of the most important natural resources in the world today. Most petroleum comes from oil wells in the United States, the North Sea, Russia, and countries in South America and the Middle East.

Big ships or long pipelines carry petroleum from oil wells to refineries. Refineries heat petroleum and break it down to make different kinds of products. Refineries make petroleum into motor oil and fuel oil that can heat homes and run electric power plants. They make jet fuel for airplanes and diesel fuel for trucks, trains, and ships.

An oil well pump brings petroleum up from deep inside the earth.

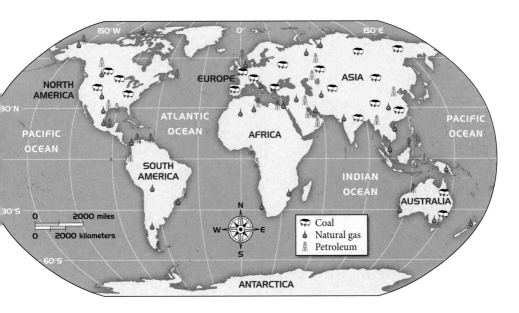

One of the most important products made at refineries is gasoline. Gasoline became an important fuel after automobiles began to replace horses in the early 1900s. The millions of cars that now zoom along the world's highways need lots of gasoline. Almost half of all the petroleum produced today is made into gasoline.

Important chemicals called petrochemicals also come from petroleum. Petrochemicals are raw materials for fertilizers and bug killers that farmers spray on their crops. Petrochemicals also make laundry detergents and furniture polish. Most plastics come from petroleum. Even some of your clothes are cut from nylon, rayon, and other fabrics made from petrochemicals.

A map showing the locations of major deposits of fossil fuels throughout the world

The Rise of Petroleum

People have used petroleum for thousands of years. The ancient Egyptians and Babylonians used pitch, which is a solidlike form of petroleum that seeped up to the surface of the earth. Native Americans burned oil for fuel long before Europeans arrived. Native Americans skimmed oil that had bubbled up to the surface of certain lakes and streams. They used the oil to make their canoes waterproof and to treat frostbite.

Petroleum did not become important as a natural resource until kerosene was discovered in the mid-1800s. Kerosene was a fuel that could be distilled from coal or crude oil. There were no electric lights at that time. People lit their homes at night with lamps that burned oil made from whales, fish, or plants. Kerosene was a much better fuel for lamps.

Another important event occurred in 1859. An American named Edwin L. Drake used a steam engine to drill an oil well in Pennsylvania. Others soon began drilling oil wells. Refineries were built to distill kerosene from the crude oil.

Oil wells and oil refineries became big businesses in the 1900s, after automobiles were invented.

Edwin Drake (right, in top hat) in front of his oil well in Titusville, Pennsylvania, in 1860

HOW DO WE USE NATURAL GAS?

Geologists drill wells in rock to reach the natural gas. Long pipes carry natural gas from the wells to storage tanks. Other pipes carry the gas to your house. Gas stoves, gas clothes dryers, and gas furnaces work by burning natural gas.

FAST FACT: In its pure state, natural gas has no smell. As a safety measure, companies add a chemical to the gas that smells like rotten eggs. That way you can always smell a gas leak.

A flame on a stove powered by natural gas

CHAPTER FIVE

Conserving Fossil Fuels

WHAT WOULD HAPPEN if we ran out of fossil fuels? Try to imagine life without gasoline to power the family car. Imagine no fuel for trains, trucks, or airplanes. What if power plants could not generate electricity because they had no fuel?

Conservationists are studying ways to avoid such a disastrous situation. They design and promote recycling programs that extend Earth's resources. Recycling plastic bottles and bags saves petroleum, which is the raw material used to make those products. Recycling also helps conserve energy that would be used to process raw materials.

Materials for recycling are left out for pickup.

Urban planners look for ways to increase public transportation, which saves on driving and gasoline use. Industry leaders look for ways to improve wasteful mining and manufacturing practices. Engineers design new cars, furnaces, refrigerators, and other machines that use less fuel and give off less pollution.

You can help conservation efforts by making small changes at home. Using less hot water, lowering the thermostat, and turning off unnecessary lights will save fossil fuels.

FAST FACT: If you could stack up all the gasoline-burning cars and vans in the United States—bumper to bumper—they would go up to the moon and back to Earth.

New York City's subways take about 120 million fares a month, saving millions of gallons of gasoline use.

FUEL-EFFICIENT CARS

Making automobiles that burn less gasoline is one of the best ways to conserve petroleum. Engineers are designing auto bodies and engines that weigh less than those of older cars. Lighter cars use less gas. Designers are also trying to build engines that burn less gasoline.

One new type of car is called the hybrid. It is powered by both a gasoline engine and an electric motor. Electric-only cars were first invented in the late 1800s. They run on batteries and cannot go very fast or very far. The batteries are difficult to recharge. You can't pull a car into a service station and say, "Charge her up, please."

In a hybrid car, the batteries get charged as the car moves along. Energy from stopping the car also helps recharge the batteries.

A hybrid sometimes draws power only from the electric motor and sometimes only from the gasoline engine. Sometimes the motor and the engine work together for greater power. As a result, hybrids can get at least 20 miles per gallon (8 kilometers per liter) more than regular automobiles.

The Toyota Prius was one of the first hybrid cars.

CHAPTER SIX

⊕ Alternative Energy Sources

IF WE CONTINUE using petroleum at current levels, experts guess that we will start running out in about 50 years. Conservation could increase the life of petroleum supplies by as much as 200 years. But what then? One answer is alternative energy. Alternative energy sources are ways of making energy without fossil fuels or nuclear fission.

WATER AND WIND POWER

People have used water and wind power for thousands of years. Today, water falling over hydroelectric dams drives machines that make electricity.

The Shasta Dam in northern California creates the world's largest man-made waterfall.

Windmills can run machines that make electricity in places where strong winds blow. Near cities such as Palm Springs, California, you can see acres and acres of windmills that are generating electric power.

Scientists are also looking for ways to harness the power of the oceans to produce energy. In France and Russia, they have built barriers like dams across bays. As water rushes in at high tide or rushes out at low high tide, it falls over the dam. The falling water drives machines that produce electricity.

The power of wind is converted into electricity at a wind farm.

SOLAR ENERGY

Engineers are experimenting with ways to harness energy from the sun. If they could harness all the energy in sunlight for just one minute, they could supply all of the world's energy needs for an entire year.

Solar panels on the roof of this house convert sunlight into usable power.

One way to harness solar energy is to collect and store energy from sunlight in water-filled panels. The energy can heat water for use in homes and office buildings. Large fields of solar collectors can store enough energy to heat water for making steam in an electric power plant.

Engineers are also trying to build more efficient solar cells. Solar cells are like batteries that can turn sunlight into electricity. Solar cells already provide electric power for spacecraft. Someday, they may provide power for ships, airplanes, and automobiles.

GEOTHERMAL ENERGY

Rocks deep inside the earth are very hot. They instantly turn any water that touches them into steam. Sometimes, the steam erupts through cracks in the ground called geysers. This energy released from inside the earth is called geothermal energy.

Geothermal energy was first used to generate electricity in Italy in 1904. Wells are drilled to tap into the geothermal heat much the way wells are drilled to reach oil.

Devices called heat pumps use geothermal energy to heat individual homes and other buildings. A heat pump can transfer heat from the ground to a house during winter. It can move the heat back into the ground during summer.

The Environment-Energy Link

Replacing fossil fuels with alternative sources of energy could protect some of Earth's other natural resources. Fossil fuels cause air and water pollution. Exhaust from gasoline burned in automobile engines causes a kind of pollution called smog.

Smoke from factories and electric power plants that burn fossil fuels can cause a kind of pollution called acid rain. Acid rain falling on lakes and rivers makes the water too acidic for fish and other animals to live in.

Automobiles, factories, and electric power plants also give off carbon dioxide gas. Carbon dioxide is called a greenhouse gas because it traps heat energy from the sun the way glass traps

Smog hovers over a busy street in Mexico City.

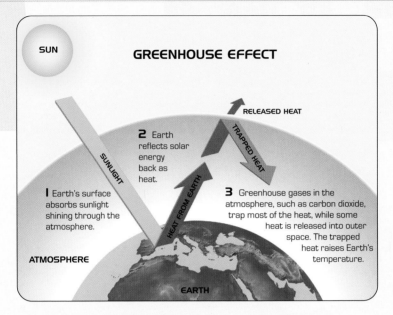

GREENHOUSE EFFECT

SUN

RELEASED HEAT

TRAPPED HEAT

SUNLIGHT

HEAT FROM EARTH

2 Earth reflects solar energy back as heat.

1 Earth's surface absorbs sunlight shining through the atmosphere.

3 Greenhouse gases in the atmosphere, such as carbon dioxide, trap most of the heat, while some heat is released into outer space. The trapped heat raises Earth's temperature.

ATMOSPHERE

EARTH

heat inside a greenhouse. The greenhouse effect is what makes Earth warm enough to support life.

Too much carbon dioxide in the atmosphere, however, could make Earth too warm. Most scientists fear that this is happening now. Since the Industrial Revolution began, burning fossil fuels have added carbon dioxide to the atmosphere. At the same time, the average temperature of the planet has been rising.

A "runaway" greenhouse effect could change Earth's climate. This global warming could melt ice caps at the North Pole and South Pole. It could cause severe flooding in some places and droughts in others. Many scientists and governments believe that we should limit the amount of carbon dioxide sent into the atmosphere by automobiles and industries.

This diagram shows how heat is accumulating in the atmosphere, causing a greenhouse effect.

BIOMASS ENERGY

Biomass fuels come from scrap wood, dried cornstalks, seaweed, other dead plants, and animal waste. Biomass fuels can be burned directly or turned into other fuels. A type of alcohol made from biomass is a cleaner-burning fuel for cars than gasoline.

FUTURE ALTERNATIVE ENERGY SOURCES

Some scientists believe that hydrogen may one day be the main fuel for automobiles. Hydrogen is found in water and in air, so we will never run out of it. It does not give off harmful pollutants, either.

This biomass power plant is burning leftover tree branches from an orchard.

The hydrogen would be used in fuel cells, which are similar to batteries. Fuel cells turn chemical mixtures into electricity. The batteries that we're familiar with run down quickly, however, and must be recharged. Fuel cells last much longer.

Other scientists are trying to produce energy from nuclear fusion, a safe kind of nuclear reaction. Unlike nuclear fission, which is the kind of nuclear power used in bombs, nuclear fusion can be easily stopped. In a fusion reaction, two atoms join, or fuse, together. This fusion gives off huge amounts of energy.

In nature, nuclear fusion reactions are what power the sun and other stars. Nuclear fusion reactors would be fueled by a type of hydrogen instead of uranium, which is nonrenewable. Physicists hope that nuclear fusion will someday replace fossil fuels in electric power plants.

WHY DON'T WE USE ALTERNATIVE ENERGY NOW?

We are using some alternative energy sources, but there are major problems with these types of energy. Hydroelectric power plants today produce more electricity than any other alternative energy source. However, hydroelectric power can be generated only where there are big enough rivers for building dams.

Biomass is the second most popular alternative energy source after hydroelectric power. Biomass fuels, however, give off some pollutants. Also, it would take all of the plants growing in

one-third of the United States to provide all the energy needs of the country.

Geothermal energy is the third most popular alternative energy source. Geothermal wells must be drilled in places where the earth's heat is close to the surface. However, these places are hard to find and access. They are often near active volcanoes.

The biggest problem with alternative energy sources is that they still cost much more than fossil fuels. Most people are not willing to pay more for alternative energy. Someday, gas and oil will be scarce, though, and the price of fossil fuels will go up. When that happens, alternative energy sources will be cheaper than fossil fuels.

Meanwhile, conserving natural resources by recycling, turning off lights when you leave a room, and driving fuel-efficient cars can help. Governments and energy companies are working hard to ensure that new kinds of energy are available before fossil fuels run out.

A geothermal power plant in Iceland

acid rain—rain, snow, or fog that contains acids made from pollutants mixing with water in the air

carbon dioxide—a greenhouse gas in air that traps heat from the sun

diesel fuel—a fuel used by diesel engines in trucks and other large vehicles; diesel fuel is heavier than gasoline

distilled—to have the impurities taken out of a liquid by heating it, collecting the gas it makes, and then letting the gas cool into a liquid again

global warming—a warming of Earth caused by too much carbon dioxide in the atmosphere

habitats—where plants or animals live in their natural states

hazardous—dangerous, particularly when relating to poisonous substances

industrialized—dependent on businesses and factories (instead of farming) as the main source of money

infertile—not able to produce crops

nuclei—the centers of atoms; *nuclei* is the plural form of *nucleus*

nutrients—substances, such as vitamins, that plants and animals need for good health

peat—layers of decayed plants

pesticide—a chemical used to kill insects and other small creatures that harm plants

photosynthesis—the process in which green plants use sunlight, water, and carbon dioxide to make food

plankton—tiny one-celled animals and algae

radioactive—being made up of atoms with nuclei that can break apart

raw materials—substances in their most natural states that are processed and used to make goods

refinery—a place where petroleum is made into gasoline, motor oil, and other products

sedimentary rock—rock that formed from hardened mud, sand, and other loose particles

swamp—low land that is often flooded

▸ Trees have always been an important natural resource in North America. Early pioneers used trees to build log cabins. They cut down trees and sawed the trunks into logs. Some Native Americans stretched animal skins over wooden poles to make the walls of tepees and lodges. Many houses today are built of wooden boards made from trees.

▸ The mixture of gases in the air is just right for supporting life on Earth. A gas called ozone high up in the atmosphere blocks harmful rays from the sun. By trapping heat from the sun, a gas called carbon dioxide makes Earth warm enough to support life.

▸ Oil companies measure crude oil in barrels. One barrel of oil is equal to 42 gallons (159.6 liters).

▸ About 25 percent of the energy used in the United States comes from natural gas. More home furnaces use natural gas than any other kind of energy.

▸ Burning natural gas gives off carbon dioxide and water vapor— the same substances that you give off when you breathe.

▸ Wyoming now produces more coal than any other U.S. state. But Montana has more coal left in the ground. Texas uses more coal than any other state.

▸ Almost all the coal used in the United States—9 out of 10 tons— is used to make electricity. Burning coal heats water to make steam. The steam turns a turbine, which drives an electric generator.

▸ The United States produces more coal than any other country. This amounts to 1 billion tons (0.9 billion metric tons) a year, which is about 35 percent of the world's coal supply.

Oil barrels from a company in Yemen, a country in the Middle East

At the Library

Parker, Steve. *Oil and Gas*. Milwaukee, Wisc.: Gareth Stevens, 2004.

Petersen, Christine. *Alternative Energy*. New York: Children's Press, 2004

Richards, Julie. *Fossil Fuels*. North Mankato, Minn.: Smart Apple Media, 2003.

Sherman, Josepha. *Fossil Fuel Power*. Mankato, Minn.: Capstone Press, 2004.

Snedden, Robert. *Energy from Fossil Fuels*. Chicago: Heinemann Library, 2001.

On the Web

For more information on **natural resources,** use FactHound to track down Web sites related to this book.

    1. Go to *www.facthound.com*

    2. Type in a search word related to this book or this book ID: **0756508568**.

    3. Click on the *Fetch It* button.

FactHound will find the best Web sites for you.

On the Road

Drake Well Museum
    205 Museum Lane
    Titusville, PA 16354
    814/827-2797
    www.drakewell.org
    To visit the first oil well ever drilled

Ocean Star Offshore Drilling Rig and Museum
    Pier 19
    Galveston, TX 77553
    409/766-STAR (7827)
    www.oceanstaroec.com
    To see artifacts from the daily operations of the oil business aboard a retired drilling rig

Kentucky Coal Mining Museum
    231 Main St.
    Benham, KY 40807
    606/848-1530
    www.kingdomcome.org/museum
    To learn about the history of coal mining in Kentucky